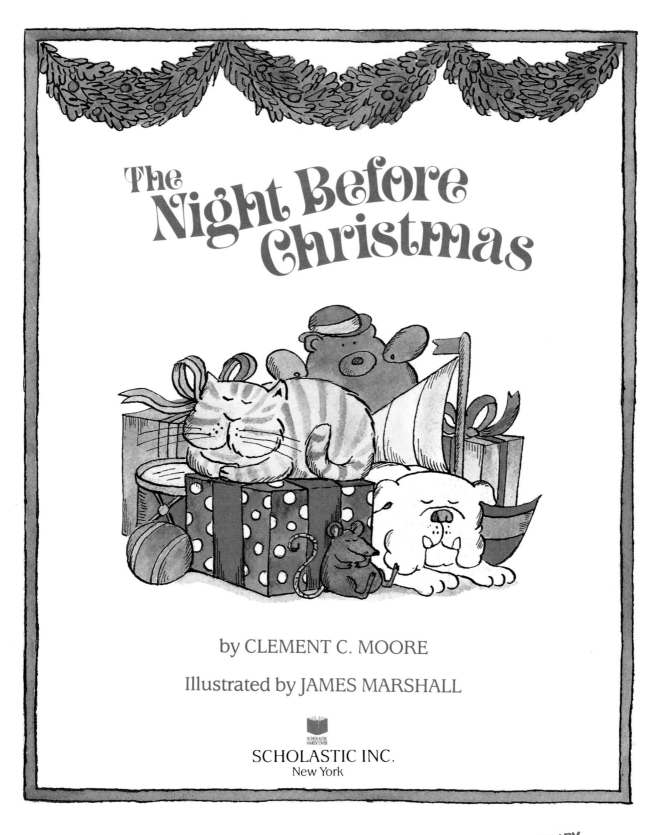

The Night Before Christmas

by CLEMENT C. MOORE

Illustrated by JAMES MARSHALL

SCHOLASTIC INC.
New York

Library of Congress Cataloging in Publication Data
Moore, Clement Clarke, 1779–1863.
The night before Christmas.
SUMMARY: The well-known poem about an important
Christmas Eve visitor.
1. Santa Claus—Juvenile poetry. 2. Christmas—
Juvenile poetry. 3. Children's poetry, American.
[1. Santa Claus—Poetry. 2. Christmas—Poetry.
3. American poetry. 4. Narrative poetry] I. Marshall,
James, 1942–   ill.   II. Title.
PS2429.M5N5   1985   811'.2   85-2144

ISBN 0-590-45075-1

12 11 10 9 8 7 6 5 4 3 2 1   10   1 2 3 4 5 6/9
Printed in the U.S.A.   36

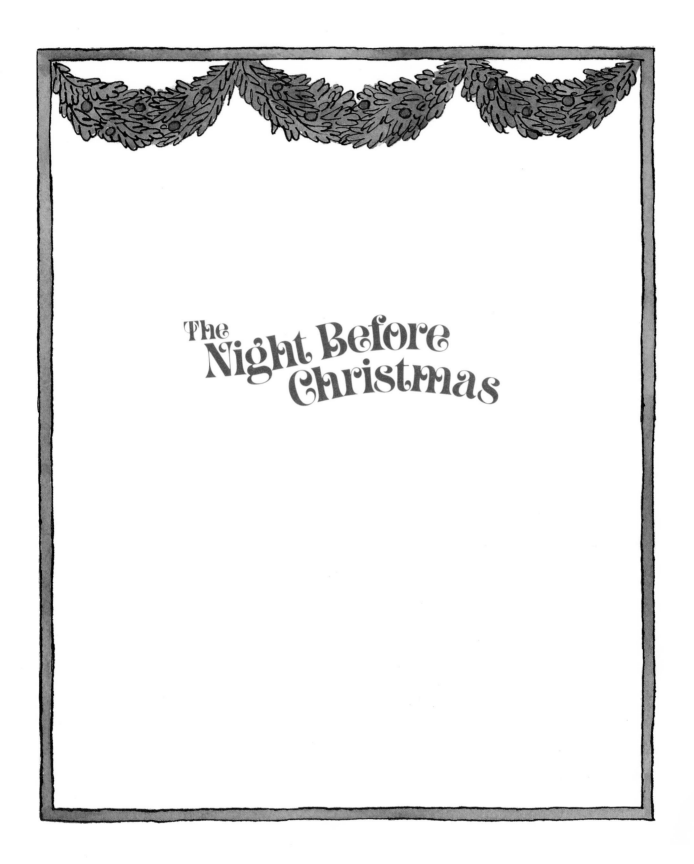

The Night Before Christmas

'Twas the night before Christmas,
when all through the house
Not a creature was stirring,
not even a mouse;

The stockings were hung
   by the chimney with care,
In hopes that St. Nicholas
   soon would be there;

The children were nestled
all snug in their beds,
While visions of sugarplums
danced in their heads;

And Mamma in her 'kerchief,
  and I in my cap,
Had just settled our brains
  for a long winter's nap;

When out on the lawn
    there arose such a clatter,
I sprang from the bed
    to see what was the matter.

Away to the window
    I flew like a flash,
Tore open the shutters
    and threw up the sash.

The moon on the breast
   of the new-fallen snow,
Gave the lustre of midday
   to objects below,

When, what to my wondering
   eyes should appear,
But a miniature sleigh
   and eight tiny reindeer,

With a little old driver,
   so lively and quick,
I knew in a moment
   it must be St. Nick.

More rapid than eagles
   his coursers they came,
And he whistled, and shouted,
   and called them by name;

"Now, Dasher! Now, Dancer!
   Now, Prancer and Vixen!
On, Comet! On, Cupid!
   On, Donder and Blitzen!

To the top of the porch!
   To the top of the wall!
Now dash away! Dash away!
   Dash away all!"

As dry leaves that before
   the wild hurricane fly,
When they meet with an obstacle,
   mount to the sky;

So up to the housetop
   the coursers they flew,
With the sleigh full of toys,
   and St. Nicholas too.

And then in a twinkling,
   I heard on the roof,
The prancing and pawing
   of each little hoof—

As I drew in my head,
   and was turning around,
Down the chimney St. Nicholas
   came with a bound.

He was dressed all in fur,
   from his head to his foot,
And his clothes were all tarnished
   with ashes and soot;

A bundle of toys
   he had flung on his back,
And he looked like a pedlar
   just opening his pack.

His eyes—how they twinkled!
   His dimples, how merry!
His cheeks were like roses,
   his nose like a cherry!

His droll little mouth
   was drawn up like a bow,
And the beard of his chin
   was as white as the snow;

The stump of his pipe
   he held tight in his teeth,
And the smoke it encircled
   his head like a wreath;

He had a broad face
    and a little round belly,
That shook when he laughed,
    like a bowlful of jelly.

He was chubby and plump,
    a right jolly old elf,
And I laughed when I saw him,
    in spite of myself,

A wink of his eye
    and a twist of his head,
Soon gave me to know
    I had nothing to dread;

He spoke not a word,
   but went straight to his work,
And filled all the stockings;
   then turned with a jerk,

And laying his finger
    aside of his nose,
And giving a nod,
    up the chimney he rose;

He sprang to his sleigh,
    to his team gave a whistle,
And away they all flew
    like the down of a thistle.

But I heard him exclaim,
  ere he drove out of sight,
"Happy Christmas to all.
  And to all a good night."

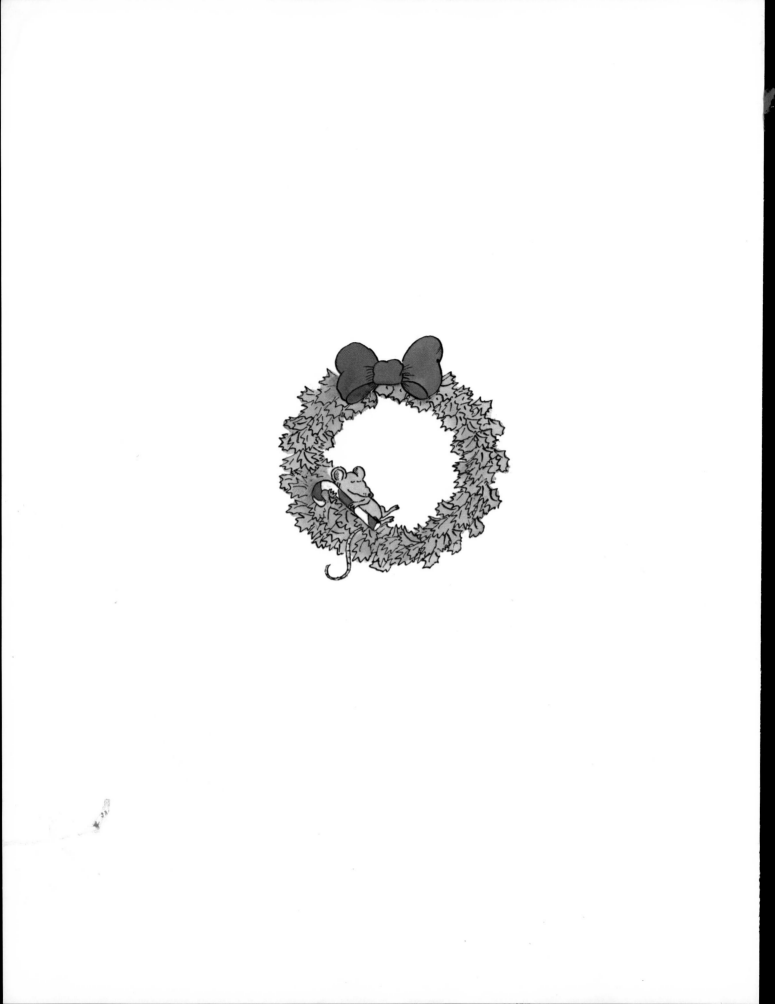